A MARITIME MOSAIC

Photography by Wayne Barrett & Anne MacKay

NIMBUS
PUBLISHING

Nimbus Publishing Limited
P.O. Box 9301, Station A
Halifax, NS   B3K 5N5
(902) 455-4286

Design: Kate Westphal, Graphic Detail
Charlottetown, PEI

Printed and bound in Hong Kong

Canadian Cataloguing in Publication Data
Barrett, Wayne.
A Maritime mosaic.
ISBN 1-55109-202-6
1. Maritime Provinces—Pictorial works.
I. MacKay, Anne. II. Title.
FC2028.B37 1997   971.5'04'0222   C97-950001-X
F1035.8.B37 1997

Acknowledgements
We wish to thank the following individuals for their generous assistance in the production of *A Maritime Mosaic:* Kate Westphal for her graphic design and layout; Joanne Elliott and Dorothy Blythe of Nimbus Publishing for their contribution in planning and production. A special thanks to Frank and Joan Ricketts, Cary Vollock, and Charmaine Gaudet for their generous hospitality. Thanks to Audrey and Donald MacKay for providing attentive care of our children while we were away from home working on this project. Last but not least, thanks to the countless Maritimers who have graciously shared with us their special places.

The infamous Bay of Fundy fog blankets the headlands at Fundy National Park, NB.

*An inverted dory overlooks the
Northumberland Strait at
Cap–Lumière, NB.*

*Overleaf left: Car lights form a ribbon
of red up the mountainside of Cape
Rouge in the Cape Breton Highlands
National Park, NS.*

*Overleaf right: Looking out over the
dunes in Springbrook, PEI.*

INTRODUCTION

While the pull of the moon affects the tides, so too, does the Atlantic beckon Maritimers home from away—a palpable tug that is felt strongly in the heart. It may be cliché to mention the influence of the mercurial Atlantic on the Maritime Provinces, but when a presence is as permanent as it is changeable, it is impossible to ignore. The three provinces that make up the Maritimes—New Brunswick, Nova Scotia, and Prince Edward Island—suffer the misconception that the region is merely impoverished, deprived of the urban prosperity known to central and western Canada. True, development in the Maritimes has moved at its own pace; however, most Maritimers would argue strongly that there is recompense for staying close to home. The images presented here subtly suggest the reasons for such diehard devotion to a region that is rugged and unforgiving, yet beautiful and bountiful.

The Maritimes, covering just over one per cent of Canada's territory, is a mosaic of landscapes, cultures, and traditional ways of life, united by the distinct influence of the sea. With so little area to its name, the variations in wondrous landscape are surprising. Terrain from forest to pasture, mountain to valley is embraced by the long and jagged coastline carved by the waves of the Atlantic Ocean and Bay of Fundy, and shaped through time. The fertile Saint John River Valley, prime potato cropland in New Brunswick, and the busy ice-free port at Saint John mark the contrasts between rural and urban influence. In Nova Scotia, the rugged coastline is never far from sight, granting spectacular panoramic vistas from Blomidon Look-off or from the windswept granite coast at Peggys Cove. The sea-sculpted red sandstone banks and winding red clay roads of Prince Edward Island are as renowned as Anne of Green Gables.

The ocean's many moods, as harsh as they can be serene, determine much about the atmosphere in the region. Maritime life revolves around the ocean—its industries and its pleasures. Early settlement, from aboriginal nations to European and American immigrants, was dictated according to where people could best eke out a living to support families and communities. The pattern of coastal villages and city centres in the Maritimes is telling. From quiet rural fishing villages to bustling urban areas, populations are concentrated around harbours, ports, along the ocean or on rivers, or in fertile valleys where the earth's gifts are nurtured by the arms of the sea. The weather here, which is reliably unpredictable, governs everything from work to casual conversations to friendly exchanges between strangers.

Maritimers have earned a reputation for warm hospitality and open friendliness. Perhaps the ocean teaches caring through its unsentimental ways. The pace of living here is relaxed, not frantic, and priorities begin with family and community. The hands of ancestors who farmed, fished, mined, and built, also planted the deep roots for traditional ways of life and social values. New Brunswick's early economy was based on lumbering and trade. With most of the province covered in forest and ready access to trade routes, it was a booming business. In Nova Scotia, the fisheries, agriculture, and steel and coal mining were leading industries. On Prince Edward Island, agriculture and fishing were the staples of the economy. During the age of sail in the seventeenth century, the entire Maritimes saw profits from shipbuilding, but economies began to lag with the reckless pace of industrialization in the late nineteenth century: The widespread use of steel rapidly closed traditional wooden

boat-building shops. Today, urban centres are expanding and service industries, such as tourism, are growing apace, although the traditional ways of life that have shaped the Maritimes are never far from one's senses.

A strong pot of tea and kitchen table conversations are another claim to Maritime fame, however stereotypical. Nonetheless, people do congregate in the kitchen, the same centre for enjoying celebrations as for grieving tragedies. And strong tea is often the drink for sobering and for solace. Ceilidhs and folk festivals, perhaps more popular than ever, honour the tradition of fiddle music and Gaelic lyrics, step dancing and the Highland Fling. Songs recount stories of shipwrecks and colourful sea shanties, hard times and pride of place, and the mighty sea that is at once robber and provider.

Just as the land and tradition shape the Maritimes, so, too, does cultural diversity. Officially bilingual New Brunswick has a strong French presence in the northern part of the province, close to Quebec. Acadian and aboriginal communities endure in all three provinces, despite ruthless attempts to override them with the influx of Europeans. British influences reach far and wide across the Maritimes, from the Saint John River Valley, NB, to the Cape Breton Highlands, NS, to Charlottetown, PEI. Place names, heritage, and traditions bear the distinctive marks of different cultures. Quirky expressions enliven the language, regardless of dialect; and there are at least as many dialects as there are counties in the three provinces.

There is something deeper than fate in the Maritimes that enticed early settlers to pioneer and carve villages from the forests and fields. It is more like a haunting ancestral need for

the tang of salt air on the tongue, the sound of the surf in the ears, and it continues to hold contemporary Maritimers here.

This photographic collection speaks about what Maritimers yearn for when they leave, what we appreciate about home: the sea, the shores, the unspoiled green spaces, which give comfort and inspire pride. Home and family are the ties that burn like a beacon for those who connect deeply with the area, as most Maritimers do. The essence of these three seafaring provinces is captured in *A Maritime Mosaic*, revealing a unique region where nature reigns supreme: miles of rugged ocean-carved shorelines and headlands, corrugated sand bars exposed by the ebb of tide, rolling green hills that stretch to the blue horizon, and silky sable dunes that edge sprawling beaches. Dramatic tides at the Bay of Fundy National Park, NB; striking fall foliage along the Cabot Trail in Cape Breton, NS; tropic-like beaches at Cavendish, PEI, show the spectrum of what the Maritimes are all about.

Elephant Rock, a natural wonder near Norway, PEI, is a popular Island tourist attraction.

Facing page: Rising early morning mist creates a golden glow at the mouth of Charlottetown Harbour, Keppoch, PEI.

Acadia University in Wolfville, NS.

Facing page: World famous Peggys Cove, NS, is perfectly reflected in its pristine harbour.

The sun sets over a traditional fishing weir on Campobello Island, NB.

Facing page: Friends study an old dulse-harvesting dory in Dark Harbour on Grand Manan Island, NB.

The rising sun casts its warm rays on a pebbled beach at Black Rock, Cape Breton Highlands National Park, NS.

Facing page: A view of Alexander Graham Bell's estate, Beinn Bhreagh, from the 18th hole of the Bell Bay Golf Course in Baddeck, Cape Breton, NS.

The new Confederation Bridge spans the Northumberland Strait, joining Prince Edward Island and New Brunswick.

Facing page: The waterfront in Summerside, P.E.I.

Saint John, NB, where the first United Empire Loyalists landed in 1783.

Facing page: Colourful entranceways on Germain Street in Saint John, NB.

Apple trees in South Melville, PEI.

Facing page: PEI's rich, red soil is beautifully illustrated here, in Tea Hill.

The ocean discloses one of its many moods as the sun dips below the horizon in Presqu'ile, Cape Breton, NS.

Facing page: Sea gulls wait for fishing boats to return with the day's catch in Ballantynes Cove, Cape George, NS.

Salt cod drying on a weathered fishing shed brings back memories of a once-thriving fishing industry on PEI.

Facing page: Fishermen spread their nets in the twilight, Cousins Shore, PEI.

Spring trees proudly display new leaves on the banks of the St. John River, NB.

Facing page: The world record tides of the Bay of Fundy have shaped these magnificent sculptured rock formations at Hopewell Cape, NB.

The last light of day illuminates a dory shop in Lunenburg, NS, home of the renowned schooner Bluenose.

Facing page: Five Islands, near Parrsboro, NS, is yet another example of the geological wonders found in the Bay of Fundy.

A bird's-eye view of popular Peake's Quay, Confederation Park, and Charlottetown Harbour, PEI.

Facing page: Province House, the birthplace of Canada's Confederation, is located at the end of historic Great George Street in Charlottetown, PEI.

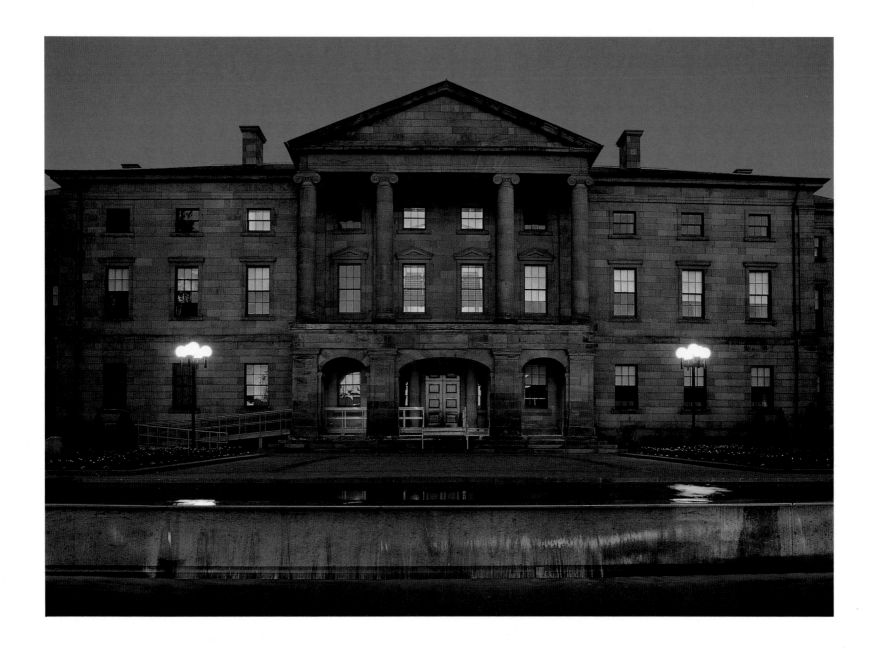

The Cape Enrage lighthouse adds to the spectacular view of the Bay of Fundy, NB.

Facing page: A colourful Atlantic puffin on Machias Seal Island, NB.

A stream of colourful light is created as cars zip along the Angus L. MacDonald Bridge in Halifax, NS.

Facing page: The Halifax skyline is majestically reflected onto the harbour.

Barachois, NB, boasts the oldest wooden Acadian church in North America.

Facing page: Carving the final touches on a wooden broom at the eighteenth-century Acadian Village near Caraquet, NB.

A horse meanders in the sun, James River, NS.

Facing page: Apples ripe for the picking in Lower Canard, Annapolis Valley, NS.

Harvesting Irish moss the old-fashioned way in Skinners Pond, PEI.

Facing page: The Sand Spit in Cavendish National Park, PEI.

A crimson sky fades over a North River farm, NS.

Facing page: One of the many beautiful waterways that make Kejimkujik National Park a canoeist's paradise, NS.

A young boy fishes for perch at Kings Landing Historical Settlement, NB.

Facing page: The beautiful St. John River as viewed from an inn in Gagetown, NB.

Dairy cattle graze in a lush meadow in Antigonish County, NS.

Facing page: Early autumn frost has turned a blueberry field to crimson in New Salem, NS.

The thriving city of Moncton, NB.

Facing page: Sailboats prepare for the daily races during the five-day Lobster Festival held in mid-July, Shediac, NB.

Costumed in eighteenth-century soldier's garb, French troops parade in the courtyard of the three-storey King's Bastion at the Fortress of Louisbourg, Cape Breton, NS.

Facing page: Covering 6,700 hectares, the Fortress of Louisbourg National Historic Site is the largest ongoing historical reconstruction in North America.

Fireweed frames lush, rolling hills in Green Road, PEI.

Facing page: Highlighted by the setting sun, low tide reveals Canoe Cove's many sand bars, PEI.

The Old Town Clock on Citadel Hill, downtown Halifax, NS.

Facing page: The sun illuminates one side of a street in Pictou, NS.

The ring-necked pheasant is common throughout the Maritimes.

Facing page: A patchwork of autumn leaves in Mount Stewart, PEI.

Sea foam is a common sight on the rugged coastline along Cape Rouge in Cape Breton Highlands National Park, NS.

Facing page: Bay St. Lawrence, Cape Breton, NS.

This stoic tree is a familiar sight to those travelling through Sussex, NB, on the Trans-Canada Highway.

Facing page: A light mist lingers over the Kennebecasis River on a late summer morning, NB.

A biologist holds three young Blanding's turtles in the palm of her hand in Kejimkujik National Park, NS.

Facing page: A pale turquoise sea washes onto Queensland Beach, NS.

A quiet night in Hampton, PEI.

Facing page: Fishing boats frame this North Rustico, PEI, lighthouse, which now serves as a cottage during the summer months.

Salmon fishing at Blackville on the Miramichi River, NB.

Facing page: The morning sunshine breaks through the fog and trees at Fundy National Park, NB.

A peaceful view in Long River, PEI.

Fields of all shapes and colours wind their way towards the north shore of PEI in Park Corner.

Dawn approaches on Machias Seal Island in the Bay of Fundy, NB.

Facing page: Lobster fishermen can spot their traps easily by the size and colour of their buoys.

A fisherman adjusts the line on his tuna boat off North Lake, PEI.

Facing page: A blue heron glides to a smooth landing on the West River, PEI.

A cascading waterfall at Balmoral Grist Stream, NS.

Facing page: A dramatic surf and sky at Brier Island, NS.

The Legislature, Fredericton, NB.

Facing page: The Deer Island Ferry passes behind salmon aquaculture pens on Green Point, NB.

Ox-pulling at the Berwick County Fair, NS.

Facing page: A highlight from the Tremont County Fair's horse-pull competition, NS.

A potato field in full blossom winds its way to the sea in Victoria, P.E.I.

Facing page: A scenic gem in French River, P.E.I.

Breakers crash at Glace Bay, Cape Breton, NS.

Facing page: A right whale raises its flukes as whale watchers enjoy the moment off Grand Manan Island, NB.

An enviable view at East Point, PEI.

Facing page: Unremitting tides sculpt the Island's red sandstone shoreline near Cavendish, PEI.

A parade of sail off Louisbourg, Cape Breton, NS.

Facing page: A dramatic evening skyline at Sydney, Cape Breton, NS.

Overleaf: A snow squall hovers over North Mountain in the Cape Breton Highlands National Park, NS.